IN THE HILLS

Amba Elieff

With Illustrations by
Gabrielle Elizabeth Scarlett

Published by Queer Creek Publishing 2025
South Bloomingville, OH

If you are inspired to post images of the pages of this text
on social media, please tag @amba.elieff. I would love to
witness you on your journey.

IN THE HILLS

This poetry was inspired by Southeastern Ohio. Specifically the Hocking Hills region. From the first time I visited 25 years ago, I knew that this was the place I wanted to be for the rest of my life. I have been chasing that dream ever since then. I do have my cabin in the woods where I will one day live full time. It is that dream that has helped me through a lot of life's challenges. This poetry is my way of showing my love of the land, people, wonder, and history of this region.

Galloway
"I've never seen a more beautiful place. I feel I belong to this land, rather than it belonging to me. I admire the Shawnees for having picked this spot for their Chalah-gawtha. It's a land a man might willingly die for."

Tecumseh
"...I ask only that you care for it as those before you cared for it and loved it."
Allan W. Eckert, Tecumseh!

IN THE HILLS

CONTENTS

ACKNOWLEDGEMENTS

For Diane Welch and Timothy Seewer

THE LAND

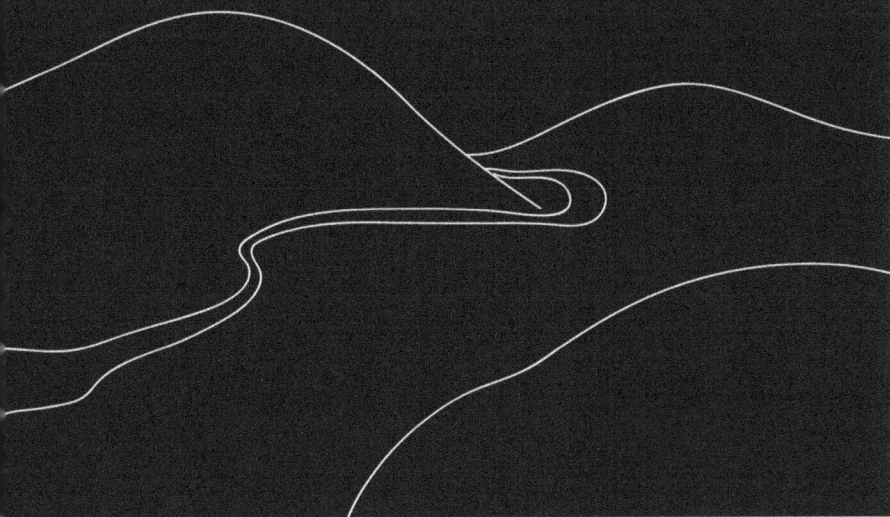

IN THE HILLS

IN THE HILLS

Grateful
that I have found
my home
in Southeastern Ohio
the land, the waters, the wildlife
I am blessed to have
a piece of land here
this is my time to honor it
I will take care of it
as long as I live
and
I will pass it to my children
to take care of it
after me

caretakers of
generational land

~ amba elieff

IN THE HILLS

Let me close my eyes
at the end of a day
in the hills
doors and windows open
breezes blow in
scent of pine
and clean
air has no unnatural smell here
and I hear a barred owl
who cooks for yoooou
calling in the trees
marking his territory
looking for dinner
as I drift off to sleep

~ amba elieff

We watched
as the outside
came to our home
our sacred places
trees
and plants
and animals
and rocks
we could not protect
from the outside
I am so sorry

~ *amba elieff*

I tentatively, reverently
touch the earrings
soft and smooth
striped deep brown and mocha
history
this piece of white oak
once part of a dam
on the Ohio canals
built in the 1830s
submerged
until 2019
virgin timber
drowned like a witch
protected
seedlings
in the 1630s
now an earring
that reminds me
trees never really die

~ amba elieff

The bend in the creek
a deep pool of water
a perfect rock to sun on
a secret swimming hole

~ *amba elieff*

Dark black hills
shadows up ahead
looming
and
I am longing
for those hills
and the smell
that tells me
I am home

~ amba elieff

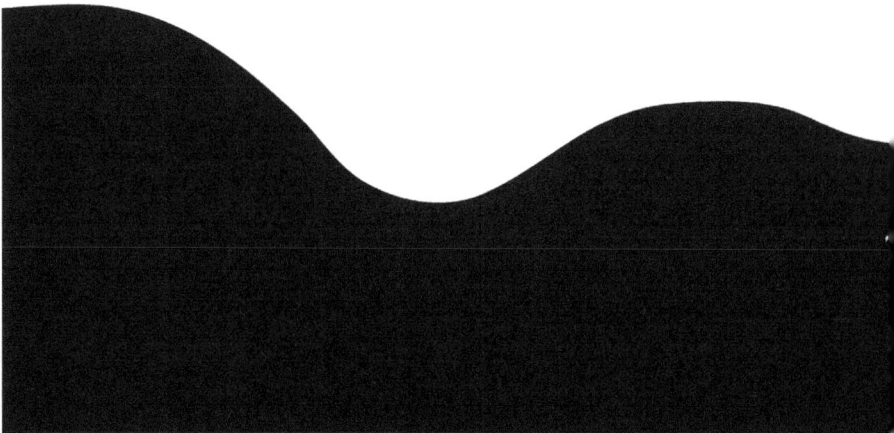

IN THE HILLS

I love driving behind farm vehicles
large wide bodies
tires as tall as my car
slowly lumbering
along the long twisty, winding roads
in the hills
roads flanked by soybean fields and corn
farmhouses and barns
sheep shorn with lambs at their sides
goats jumping and climbing on their tires
and shelters
horses lazily grazing while a colt nurses
acres of land
that ends in hills covered with forests
the constant kaleidoscope of colors
as the seasons change
I will happily sit at my 5 mile per hour pace
behind the large green behemoth
enjoying the scenery that normal driving
makes a blur
seeing things I would never see at 65 miles
an hour
I have an excuse
to go slowly
and
soak up the beauty and the oddities
there is no hurry
in the hills

~ amba elieff

Trunk
smooth and gray
tattooed by
lover's hearts
and initials
trees clinging to
their dry brown leaves
like a lost lovers embrace
well into spring

~ *amba elieff*

IN THE HILLS

This place
it is my escape
my safe space
my hide away
and oh so sacred
to me
I found myself here
during my divorce
during 9/11
during covid
during unemployment
each time my world fell apart
during every crisis
I am here
and the crisis
isn't so sharp
and painful
in this place

~ amba elieff

There is a snake
that visits my basement
I named him
Grayson
he is a black rat snake
but not black
his beautiful skin
is gray
he blends in better
with the cinder block, slate, and concrete
of the foundation
in the basement
one mild winter
my walls no longer
filled with
the sounds of mice
scurrying
and I knew
it was Grayson
and now
starting to see more
signs of mice
chewed plastic containers
mouse poop on the counters
and I wish
he would come back

~ *amba elieff*

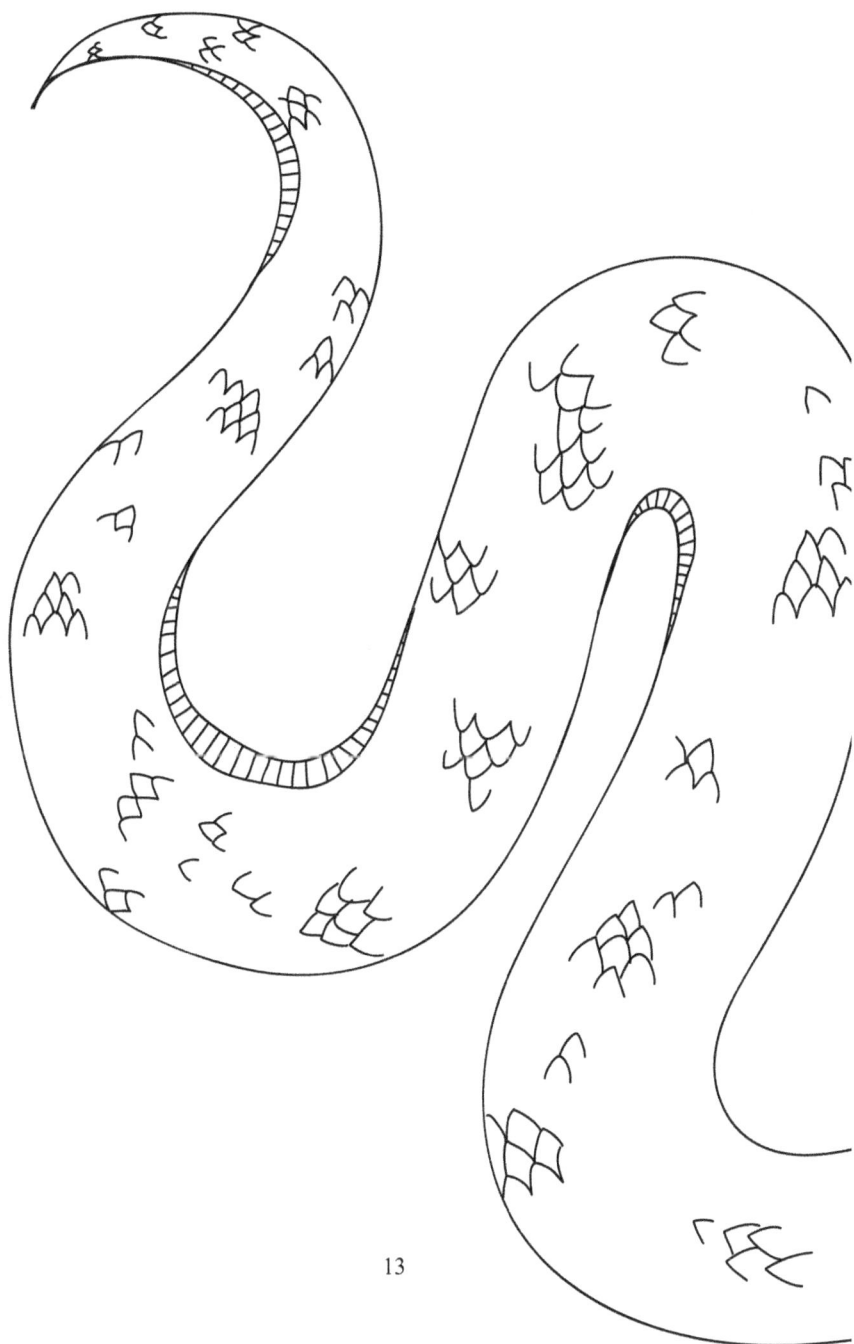

I look around at the trees
none of them more than 100 years old
in forests that I think of as forever
but they aren't
charcoal kilns once dotted
the landscape
charcoal to feed
the hungry iron furnaces

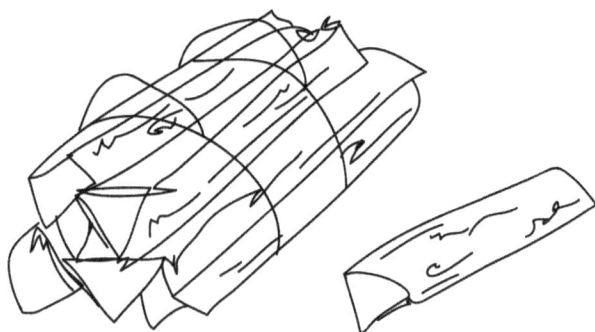

pouring out pig iron
eight to twelve tons of iron a day
ate
190 bushels of charcoal
but to make that charcoal
you burn about four cords of wood
I wonder how much that is
I start pacing off
a cord
eight feet long
four feet wide
four feet high
eight feet, sixteen, twenty-four, thirty-two
feet
up to my chest
two steps to get to the other side
every day for almost 100 years
the forests denuded in ever widening circles
until there were no trees left

~ *amba elieff*

Change
development
more and more cabins
entertainment venues
barreling into the forest
while
jack-in-the-pulpit
prays
he will still have a home

~ *amba elieff*

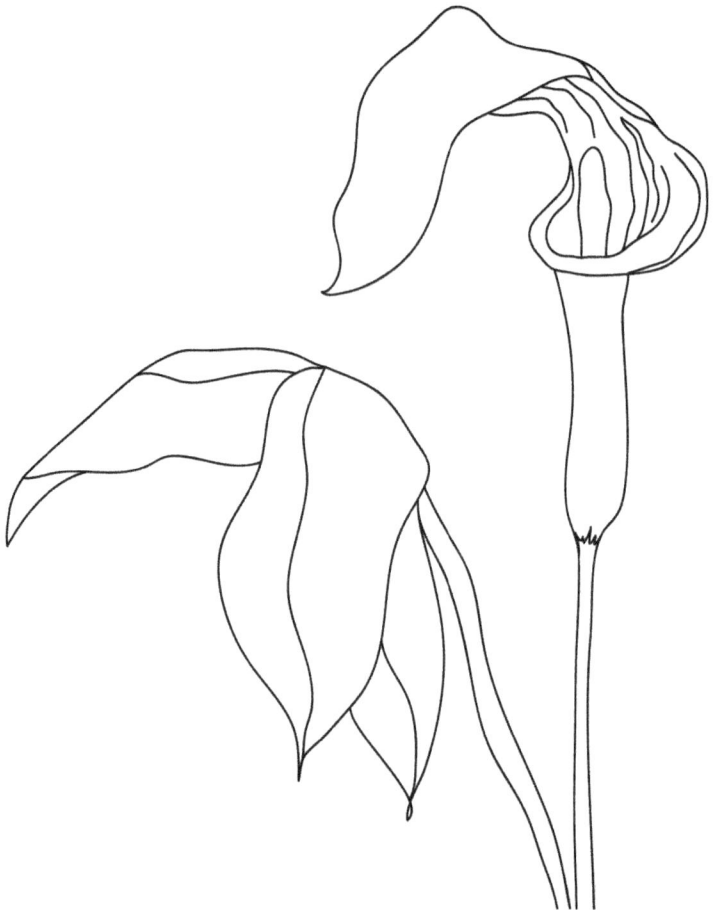

It wasn't a single feather
slipped loose
during flight
to float to the ground

clumps and puddles
of feathers
in disarray
violence
and
death

tiny
clumps of downy
feathers
innocent looking
like a babe

~ *amba elieff*

The ice building up
from the icicle up above
renegade drops collecting
one by one
til the mound of ice
becomes taller than a man
turns blue
with the excitement
reaching to touch
it's creator
the icicle up above

~ *amba elieff*

19

Spice bush is in bloom
I stare at it
from my window
blooms
look like firefly butts
golden
tiny
suspended in air
promise that spring
is here
teasing
that fireflies
will return
soon

~ *amba elieff*

Spring storms
they were coming in
rain
warnings of thunder and lightning
high winds
possible downed trees
the rain started
in the night
heavy drops
pelting the metal roof
a drum beat
and
the spring peepers
continued singing
in their vernal pool
their time to mate
the melodious sound
through the rain
their persistent song told me
that the storm
would not last long

~ *amba elicff*

I woke up
to the bullseye
on my upper right arm
plain as day
it looked like
a large dot deep pink
angry
with a circle around it
the one in nine
got me
I didn't see it
I didn't feel it
maybe it was
on one of the dogs
fell off
chose me instead
the doctor asked
if he could take pictures
he said it was classic
and he sent me home
with a month of doxycycline
and me
with my fingers crossed

~ amba elieff

Mayapples
standing tall
leaf outstretched
like a lost
pina colada umbrella

~ *amba elieff*

The branches large as full grown trees
sweep down and welcome me
like they are reaching to hold my hand
they creep along the ground
amongst the tombstones
bigger round than my body
I crawl up on a limb
and become a speck
on its massive frame
I feel the wind
you barely acknowledge the breeze
leaves high up rustle a little
and I lean into the tree
where the branch
and the trunk meet
I stare up into the leaves
and feel held
I wonder
do the people below
feel held in the roots
as the branches hold me above

~ *amba elieff*

The darkness
the perfect dark place
to stare at the sky
get lost in the milky way
see the colors
and the wash of stars
waiting
staring
trying not to blink
for the moment
the star flys
through the air
shooting toward the earth
coming to you
it disappears
more staring
waiting
for the next one

- amba elieff

We get our water
from springs and wells
springs not tested
but faithful
52 degrees
flowing from the earth
pipes tapped in
a clear cool stream
on a hot day
and wells
no city water here
wells
filled with frogs and salamanders
promising the water is safe

~ *amba elieff*

IN THE HILLS

Ghost deer
always spotted
but
white as snow in winter
small and lean
flat antlers like a moose
old world deer
come from across the ocean
to land in the hills
tucked in a corner
petting zoo
cracked corn
a quarter
a handful
children's delight
feeding the deer

~ *amba elieff*

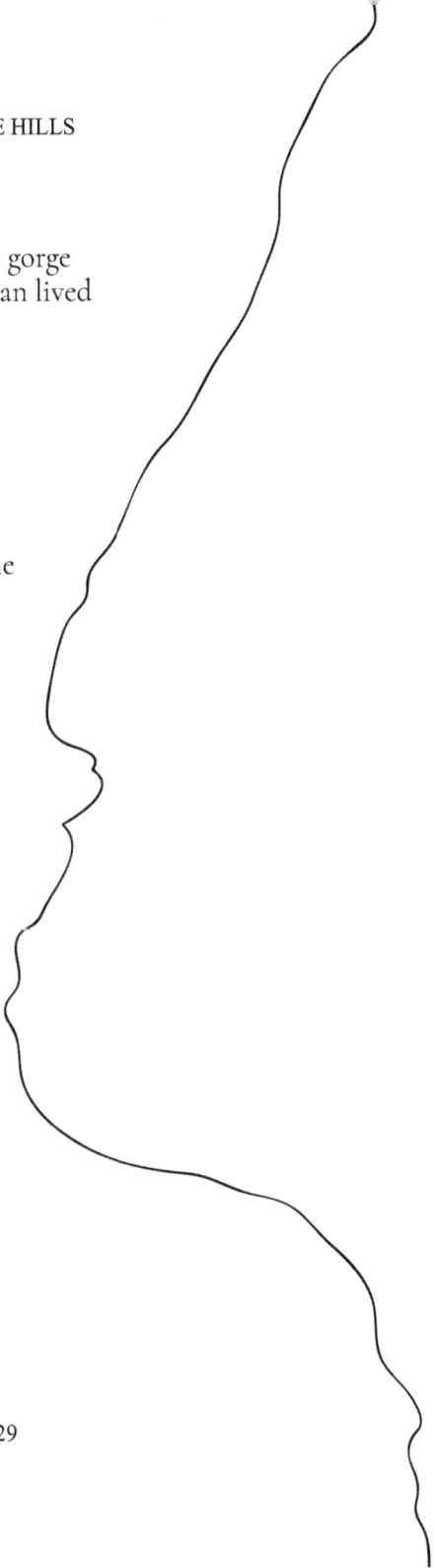

IN THE HILLS

Hiking down into the gorge
from where the old man lived
in a cave
eye spy a man's home
eye spy a sphinx head
a whale
a turtle head
in the sandstone
in the gorge
images hidden in stone
What do you spy?

~ amba elieff

Poison ivy
many years old
wraps her jungle tail
around and around
up the tree
thick as my arm
leaves and berries
high up and hidden

~ *amba elieff*

Perfect lunch spot
whispering falls
the echo from the
rock face
the long falls
crashing down
watching
as the water tumbles
into the pool
droplets flung
far and wide
and then the movement
the falls sashay slowly
left
then
they sashay slowly
right
a dance of water
only visible
it you sit still
and watch

- *amba elieff*

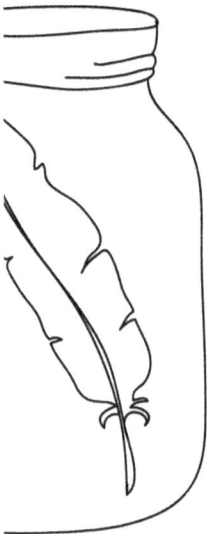

32

The feathers disappeared
I still saw birds
chirping and bouncing in the woods
but no feathers for me to find
the angels no longer watching
messaging
then
I realized
they had not left me
they sent me you

~ *amba elieff*

The water flows from the perfect
gap in the rocks above
they appear hand placed
just for the purpose
of channeling water
down the rocks
past the small cave
and over the face
of a lady
her face turned up
toward the sun
peaking into the gorge
I see her
the water streaming
over her eyes
around her nose
caressing her cheeks
as it tumbles
to the pool below

~ *amba elieff*

IN THE HILLS

The quiet
little known corner of the world
Lake Hope
like a younger sister
a red headed stepchild
overlooked
trails so sweet
they settle in you
like a piece of home
no dramatic cliffs
huge caves
there are small hidden nooks
trails that overflow with water
after a good rain
water lilies pink
spread wide fill the lake
red eared sliders sun on logs
while beaver at sunset
slap their tails
sounds like a gunshot
Canada geese nesting
if we hike around the bend
I'll give you fruit gummies, granola bar,
a bribe
to see what is around the bend

~ amba elieff

IN THE HILLS

I stare at the creek
think of streams and rivers
Where does a drop of water live?
always moving
flowing
Where does it call home?
Does it have a home?
or is it a vagabond
a nomad
wandering
searching for a puddle
lake, ocean
to call home

~ amba elieff

IN THE HILLS

Sandstone
honeycomb weathering
decorated the stone
low on the rock face
as it reached toward the sky
up high
the stone changes
you see the stacks of flapjacks
drenched in sunset
looking at you below

~ *amba elieff*

Cold
zero
below zero
I wait for all the cold
and I welcome it
for days on end
and I wait
and I watch
drop by drop
the water slows
it's dripping
til it becomes stalactites
of ice
reaching down to me
as I hike the gorge

~ amba elieff

I hear the rain
hitting the metal roof
percussion
I am snuggled in my bed
in my cabin
my body tenses
and I try to relax
but I have had leaking roofs
water rivulets that run
along the ceiling
searching for the knots
in the pine paneling
I listen to the noise
that should be soothing
a calming percussion
but I still shine the flashlight
up where the ceiling meets
the rock
that is the back wall
where they meet
a risky joint
it is dry
and the rain pelts
but the dry
lets me relax
and drift back off
to sleep

~ *amba elieff*

IN THE HILLS

The hills
were bashful this morning
hugging the thick white clouds
close to their loins
hilltops peeking out
here
peeping out there
drenched in fog
how amazing
to wear clouds
when all I can do
is disappear
into the mist

~ amba elieff

IN THE HILLS

The bird song
a different choir
than the city
so many more singers
fee bee fee bee
drink your tea
drink your tea
peter peter
meow meow
and the percussion
tap tap tapping
on a tree

~ *amba elieff*

There is never just one
I wander off trail
to get the picture
of the butterflies
spicebush swallowtails
blue and black
with drips of orange
on the outer wing
a dozen of them
flitting around and alighting
on flowers
I wade through the grass
knee high
I never feel them
until I stop

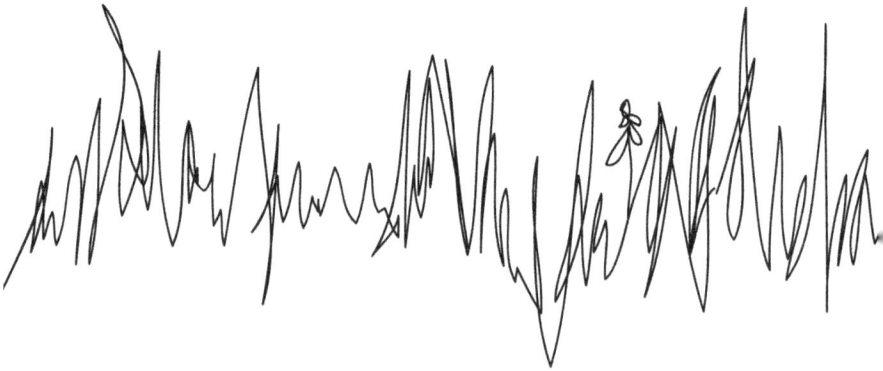

pants or shorts
a menagerie
of black dots
the size of a period
a grain of rice
a sesame seed
one the size of a pea
some decorated
with white spots
I pull them off
one by one
cut off their heads
watch the blood squirt
no time for bullseyes

~ *amba elieff*

IN THE HILLS

Everytime
I drive east
toward the hills
the first sight of them
home washes over me

~ amba elieff

Houses appear
like pimples
overnight
covering the beautiful
landscapes
meadow
woods
farmer's field
we cannot pop them
to get rid of them
more like
tumors
they dig in and stay

~ amba elieff

Deep winter
everything is frozen
day and night
the water that runs
over the hills
water oozing
from the sandstone
ice
I stare at the rockface
back of the yard
stalactites of ice
trying to touch the ground
at night
I hear the loud crack
as it breaks
too heavy to hang any longer
and the flash of light
that follows
like thunder and lightning

~ amba elieff

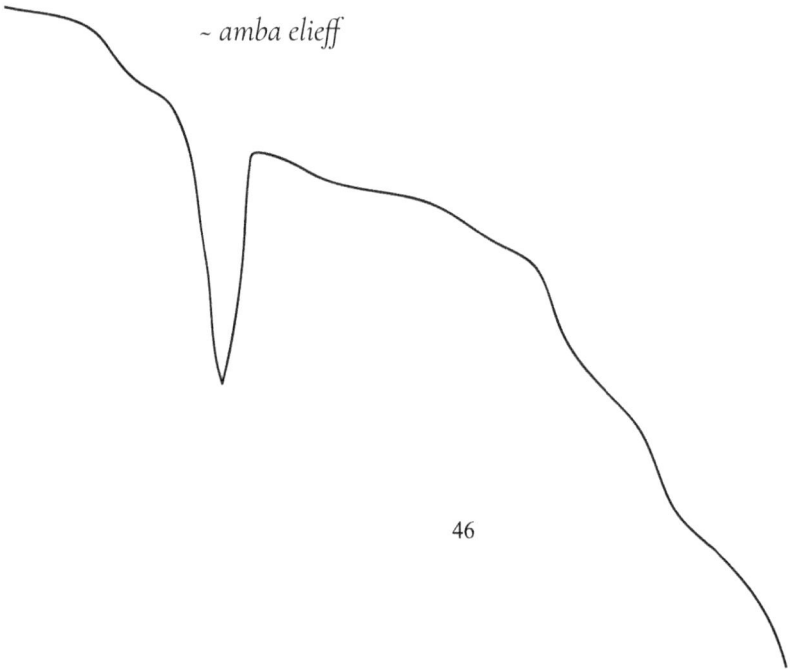

Invasives
woolly adelgid
an insect
smaller than a grain of rice
they are here
they suck the sap
from hemlocks
that is their food
we are fighting them
we still see the ghosts
of the ash trees
imagine Hocking Hills
with no hemlocks

~ amba elieff

I carry a piece
of perspective
in my pocket
a small piece
of milk quartz
reminding me
that I too can survive

~ *amba elieff*

Once upon a time
when Hocking Hills
was still a treasure
for the locals
and the few
who liked
hiking and hiding
in a place
no one knew
we crossed State Route 664
to get to Old Man's Cave
664 was between the parking
and the park
there was that little amount of traffic
there were no bathrooms
in the winter
port a potties stood guard
at the head of the trail
the visitor's center
three seasons
in the summer
the snack bar
sold hot dogs, ice cream, water
a weekend might
have the parking lot
three fourths full
days you could hike
and never see a soul
I miss once upon a time

~ *amba elieff*

I will never own this cabin
or the land, the rocks
the creek that runs below
I pay monthly
for the privilege to protect
all of it
I am merely the caretaker
we are all caretakers of this world

~ *amba elieff*

IN THE HILLS

Dew in the morning
soaks my feet
tears of mother earth
when will we start protecting her

- amba elieff

I can feel
the hills sigh
with relief
at the end of a day
grateful
when the people
finally leave
weary and licking
her wounds

- *amba elieff*

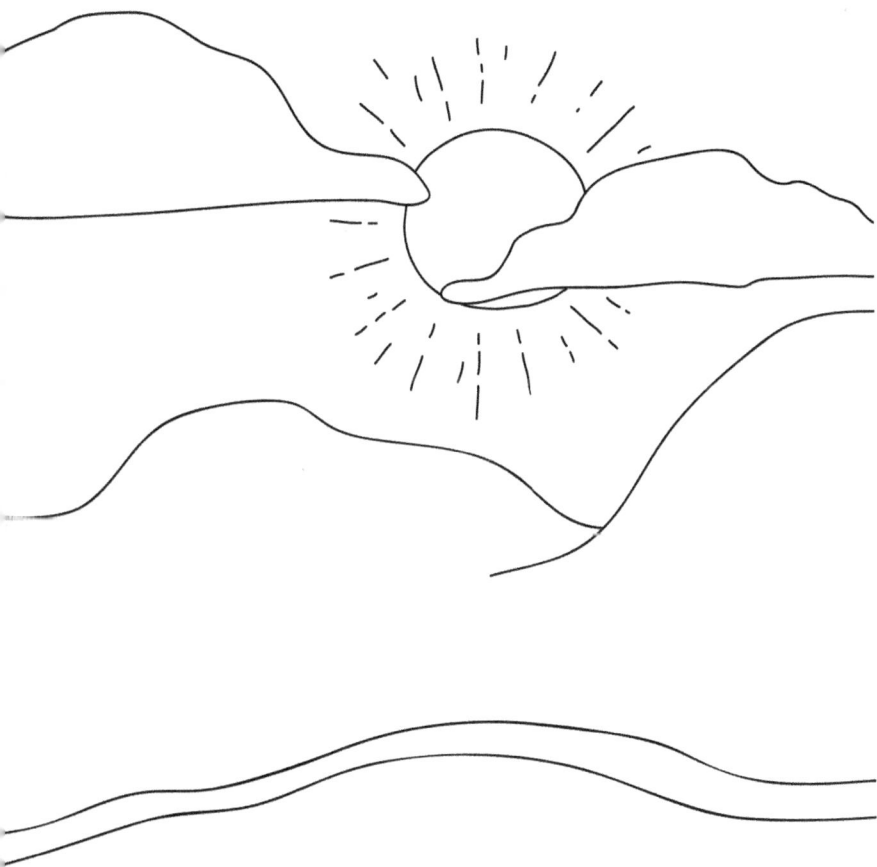

IN THE HILLS

THE PEOPLE

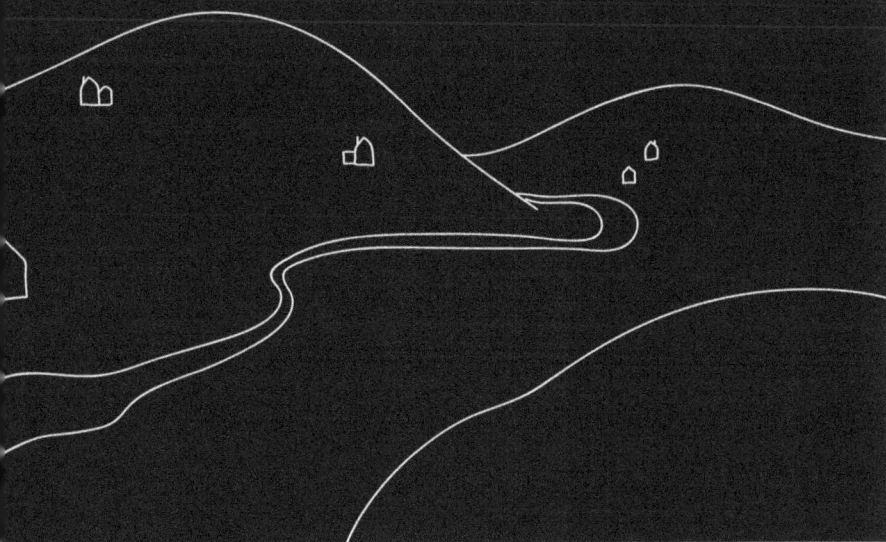

IN THE HILLS

My body
fizzed and hummed
with the energy
like electricity
and my hair standing on end
all over me
the energy of the place
no one there
but I could
feel them
their essence
all around
wanting
to share their lives

~ amba elieff

Back
and
forth
back
and
forth
my finger rubs
the rough sandstone
I stare at the pillar
I feel the grittiness of the stone
thick and solid
a tear slides down my cheek
the coolness of the shade
under the awning
and the stone
rubbing it
I steal a look down the driveway
they left me here

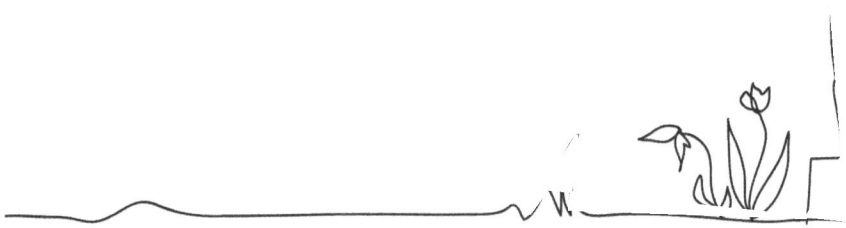

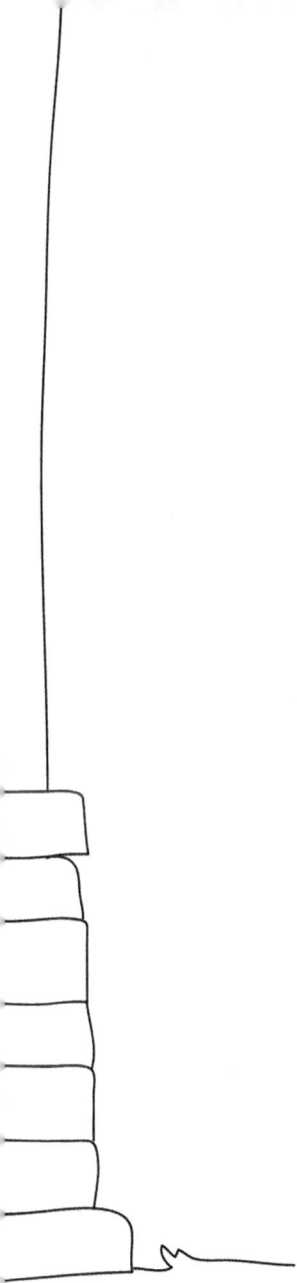

when will they return?
and my finger
strokes the stone
I wonder will I wear a groove
before I see them again
it is comforting
rubbing the stone
I count the strokes
now someone is next to me
leading me inside
I will go in for awhile, I think
then back to my stone
watching for them

~ *amba elieff*

I stare at the base of the column
thick blocks of sandstone
stacked as high as my head
cream and golden with hints of orange
supporting the awning
where my buggy is parked
the horse shifts his feet
tired of standing
as I stare at the sandstone
there are some worn spots
I wonder how they got there
I wonder if she will be happy here
I wonder if they can help her
I wonder if she will miss us
I will miss her
my finger instinctively
rubs the sandstone
a worn groove
maybe she will touch it too
and feel that I was here
thinking about her

~ *amba elieff*

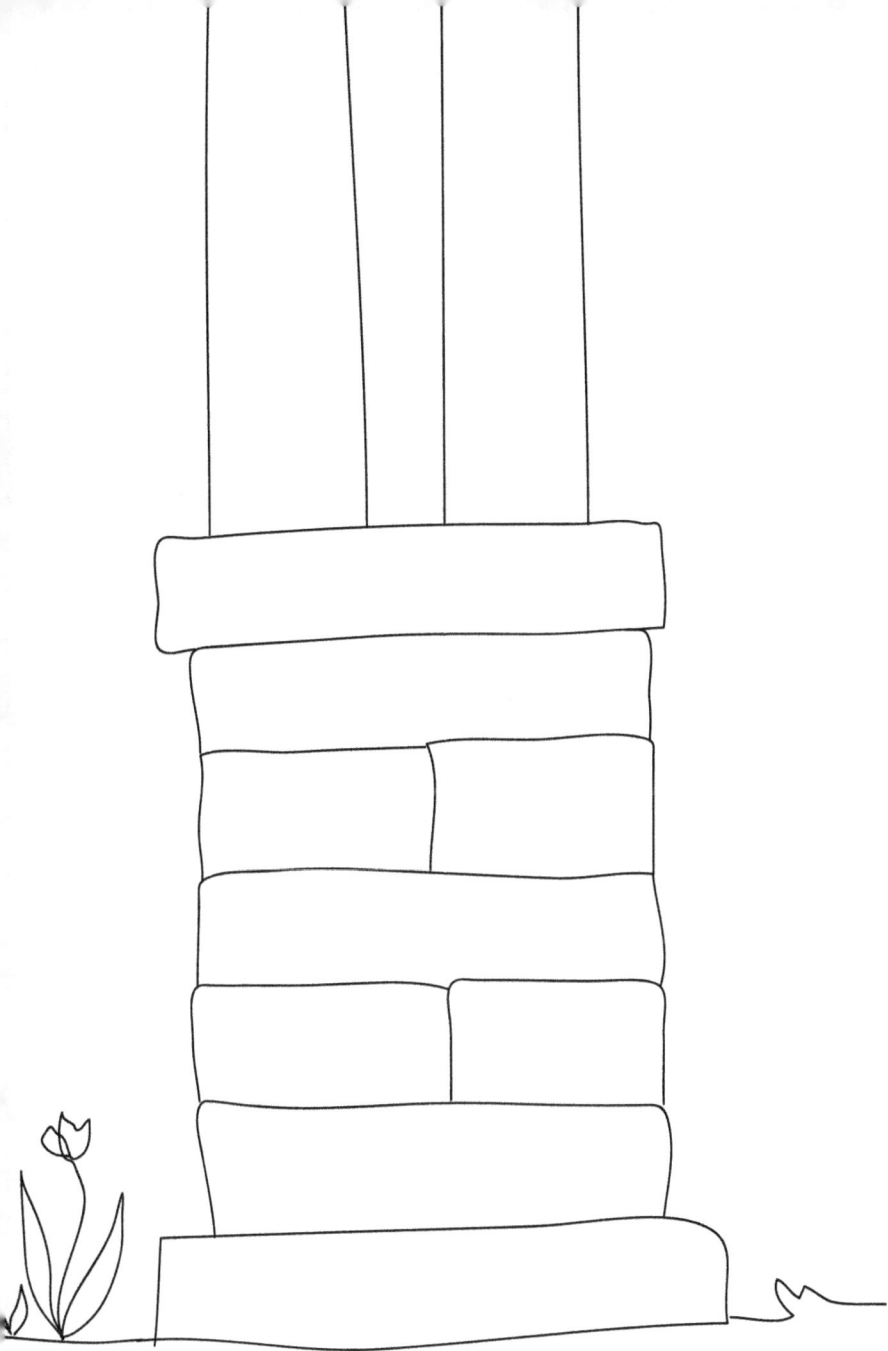

IN THE HILLS

She lived in the hills
down in a hollow
it was a beautiful place
it was a poor place
no indoor plumbing
heat from a fire
13 children
running all over
the woods and the creeks
wearing patched hand me downs
imaginary toys
she was content there
even though it was a hard life
she thinks back to her one
frivolous expense
her treasure
she loved drinking tea
never coffee
one day

at a yard sale
25 cents
a good bit of money when you have none
a delicate bone china tea pot
with big red roses
and yellow tulips
the colors were vibrant
such a cheerful little pot to look at
in the winter when the snow was knee high
the little pot filled with hot tea to warm her
belly
she bought it
her most prized possession
and her one treat
cups of tea

~ *amba elieff*
inspired by Michele Filon

I never got to visit enough
but when I did
your warmth and welcome
filled my soul
you loved artists
all types of artists
you made a place for us

everytime I visited
you sat with me
in the back with Bella
and
gave me time
to be a poet
I got to feel like a poet
not a massage therapist
scraping by
not a foolish woman
chasing a dream
everytime I dropped off
a new book
you opened it
read a few lines
here and there
head nodding
and then
you would pass
the book to me
and say
this one
and for a moment
we were two artists
sharing our lives

- *amba elieff*
inspired by Diane Welch

IN THE HILLS

So many small towns
volunteer fire departments
finally enough money
to build a firehouse
in the places where so many homes
are lost in a fire
everyone on wells
no city water
no fire hydrants
tanker trucks
2000 to 4000 gallons a tank
how many can our building hold

and two times a year
at the center of town
big yellow boots
size 14
offered to any and every car
the big boots belong to no one
they are ginormous for the offerings
no money for the volunteer firefighters
that risk their lives
but money for the tools that might
save a life or a home

~ amba elieff

A string of suckling pigs
in the sand
under the huge sandstone
blast furnace
the land is barren all around
trees taken for charcoal
burn in piles covered in dirt
there are no trees
as far as the eye can see
eaten by the needs of the furnace
the needs of the people

throwing out slag
beautiful purple
glasslike chunks of waste
the pig iron loaded
10 to 12 tons
at the end of another day

~ *amba elieff*

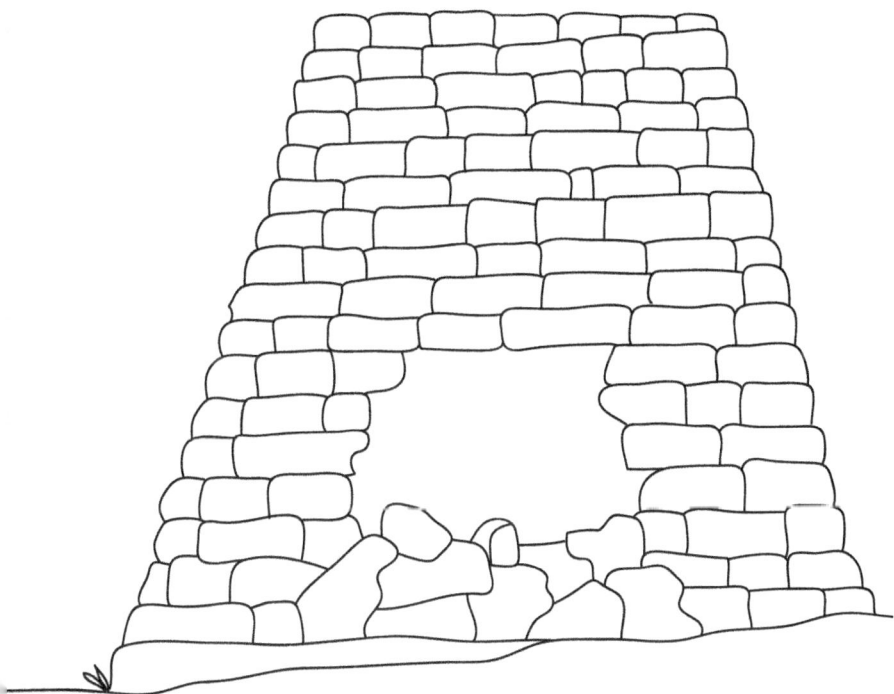

The snow was blowing outside
she stared out the windows
tall victorian
opened in 1874
the entire facility
must have been beautiful once
all the woodwork carved
now it is all painted white
she could imagine the rich wood under-
neath
the patterns of the tile
on the floor
each a mosaic
she would like to create art
like that
she looks up
at the elegant light fixtures
crown molding
intricate ironwork of the vents
the ceilings must be 14 feet high
so high from where she stands
if only she could do art
she heard art and nature were once
part of therapy here
she starts taking toilet paper
she hoards it
she finds if she makes it wet
she can turn it into something
she can sculpt
she begins to sculpt
and hide her work away
after years

she was released into the world
the toilet paper sculpting
a piece of her

she and her daughters
look out the window of their
victorian house
the snow is blowing outside
they are getting ready for Christmas
the daughters are entranced
by the six foot victorian santa
in his velvet dusky green coat
one hand holding a lantern
they put it in the front window
their mother's work
his face is sculpted of toilet paper
but to look you would never know

~ amba elieff
inspired by Shirley Farnsworth

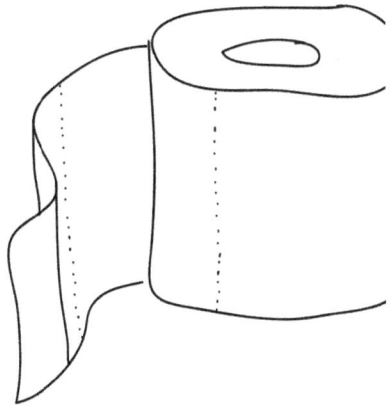

To the people who visit
we are not a place
created by humans
we are not an amusement park
there are no custodians hired
to pick up the trash
this isn't a world where
tomorrow everything
will begin again brand spanking new
like you were never here
we are a living place
created by Mother Nature
it took millions of years
for this beauty
to be born
we are a sacred place
a home for creatures
fighting to still have homes
plants
fighting to still have homes
you are visiting all our homes
respect Mother Nature
respect all of us
or
there will be nothing
left
to visit

~ *amba elieff*

The people kept coming
to see the hills
they required
space to stay
space to park
so the people
built cabins
larger and larger
and parking lots
bigger and bigger
taking down trees
and
rolling over plants
til there were no hills
left

~ amba elieff

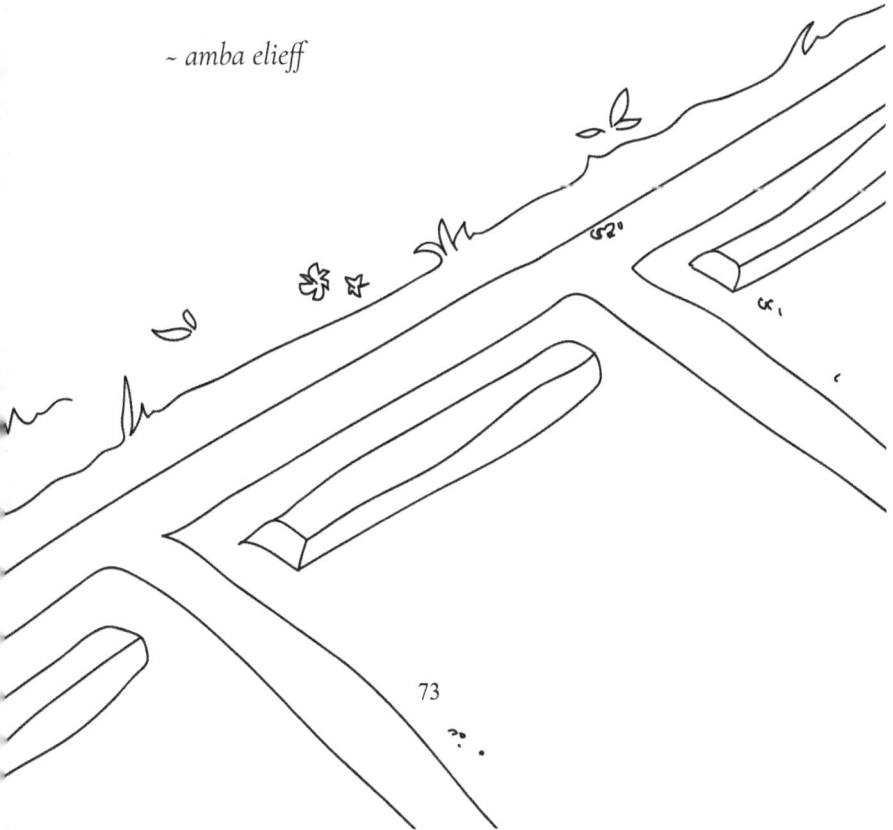

Chasing flowers
following in the footsteps
of my mentors, my heroes
they spent their lives finding and recording
and teaching and protecting and protesting
and sharing
their love of nature
teaching about habitat loss
rare and endangered plants and animals
I was in awe of them
their knowledge
and dedication

I wanted to see a pink lady's slipper
a rare flower once not so rare
a long time ago
dotting woods
they can't be moved
they require the specific fungi
in the soil to survive
and then 15 or more years for their first
flower
I so wanted to see this sacred plant in
bloom
so I asked
Where can I find it?
knowing the trust involved with sharing
this type of knowledge
and instead I got a story

a long time ago
in the hills where the biggest waterfall is
the hill sides were covered in pink lady's
slippers in the spring
Can you imagine that?
I could
it was beautiful in my mind
and devastating
because I knew they no longer existed there
then he told me
people dug them up to try to grow them at
home
they always died
they need what is in the soil
where they live
and others mindlessly
walked the hillsides
destroying the habitat and the plants
I know how barren those hillsides are now
again I saw in my mind how breathtaking
this must have been
then he smiled
and said
you will see them one day

~ amba elieff
inspired by Ralph Ramey

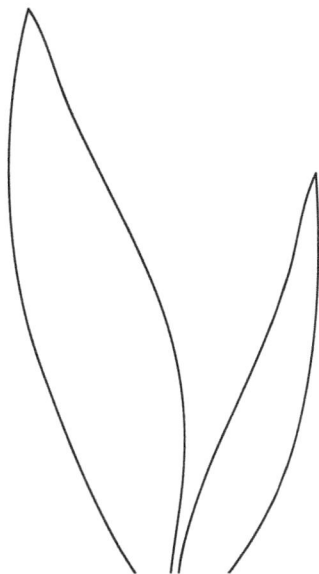

Driving on a rural state route
toward Chillicothe
my mind reviewing the list
in my head
mailboxes flashing by
I'm going to town
I need to get everything
the nearest is an hour away
no quick trips to pick up
that thing that you forgot
and I see the flashing amber lights
up ahead
the mailman
doing his deliveries
the road twists and turns
no passing zones
I relax and watch him work
when I see
the mailbox
a microwave on top of a post
an electric cord dangles down
to an outlet attached to the bottom
of the post
the mailman
opens the microwave door
inserts the mail and closes it
drives off like every other day
and as I creep forward
I smile
a microwave mailbox
only in the hills

~ *amba elieff*

She still remembers
where the still is
she thinks
kinda
she can picture it
in the woods
she could park
at the bend of the road
Grandpa's still
she closes her eyes
can see it
as large as she was at four years old
there was a grove of hemlocks
that hid the still
and the people
and the noise
they made it dark
all the time
but a still
without a recipe
is just a piece of copper

~ *amba elieff*
inspired by Missy (Waldie) Mullins

Small post office
here
in the hills
the postmaster
knows every face
every name
where they live
all their children
generations of families
generations raised together
people who care about
one another
not just know about
one another
not a city or town
where you recognize a face
you see every day
notice when you don't
but know nothing about them
won't give them a second thought
if you never see them again

~ *amba elieff*

Everyone needs
a Grandma Faye
when they run out
of bar oil
when the dog collar
breaks
when the scouts need
paracord
when you want
a local book
lunch for the trail
an odd bolt, nut, screw,
thingamajig
flashlights
firewood
batteries
barretts
blankets
tent stakes
a memory
forgot, broken, need
Grandma Faye

~ *amba elieff*

IN THE HILLS

The people kept coming
to see the hills
to hike
and
to wear the trails
and rocks
to nothingness
sand and dirt
plants no longer above ground
roots clinging below
hiding
afraid
to try to see
the light again

~ amba elieff

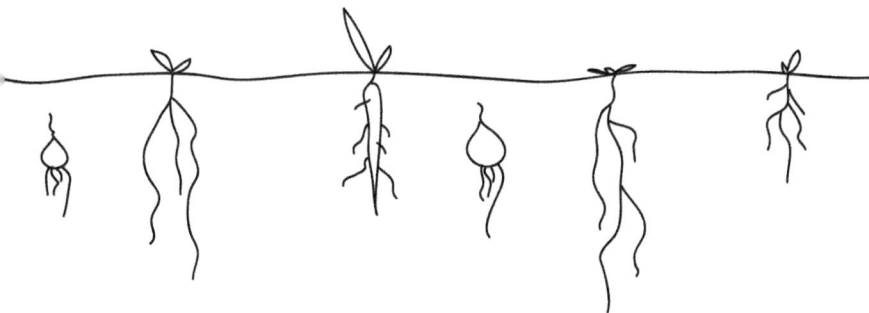

He gave me a hag stone
my first one
sandstone
worn with a perfect
circle
a hole
large enough to put
around my pinky finger
with a worn
spot that fitted
my thumb
like a worry spot
sparkles of quartz
shimmered
when I turned it in the light
thousands of years
water flowed
and made the perfect circle
he said
it was waiting for me

~ amba elieff

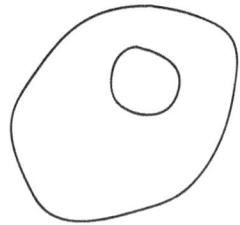

They found the quiet
no noise of a city
instead
the song of the birds
the crash of the deer
the gurgle of the creek
and the rush of the waterfalls
the call of the frogs
and it was disquieting
for them
not soothing
like the white noise of the traffic
or the regular passing of the airplanes
the random sirens
wailing
each unique ambulance, cop, fire truck
familiar sounds
the sounds of home

~ *amba elieff*

In my memory
lunchboxes
hundreds of lunchboxes
all the lunchboxes
spanning 150 years
sitting everywhere
and
we visit Mr. Etta
my daughters' name for him
lunch
veggies from his garden out back,
sauce, and soup made in his kitchen
homemade pizza, subs, soups
but he also made art - on display and for sale
and played instruments
a corner with a banjo and guitar
and an old upright piano against the wall
llamas, goats, and a donkey

in the corral outside
chickens wandering everywhere
the best place for gossip and the news
in the hills he could cover everything
check in station for deer hunters
place to grab a morning coffee and newspaper
small business owner
and though he wasn't religious
when the church up the road
needed someone to play music
he got up on Sunday mornings and played
he knew it all
and when he was gone
he was missed

~ *amba elieff*
inspired by Timothy Seewer, Etta's Lunchbox

Brass tags
a round brass disc
with numbers
simple
just a number
that is all they were
to the companies
I have the tags
tarnished brass
170, 149, 159, 129, 1485, 197
these were men who crawled
deep in the earth
to mine the coal
black as night at the end of a shift
because the mine never
stopped day and night
it is dark below ground
so day or night never mattered
the danger was always there
I hold the tags
the souls of men
sacred

~ *amba elieff*

IN THE HILLS

George picking up his mail
sliding it out of the P.O. Box
small cube in the post office wall
some of the envelopes a little crinkled
shoved in the cube a little rough
a lot of mail

Sam the postmaster
behind the counter watching
the day go by
asks about the kids
George doesn't answer
digging in his P.O. Box

George straight faced
as he walks to the counter
my mail is wrinkled
and crinkled

Sam holding a serious poker face
ironing board is set up in the back
you want me to press them for you
extra charge

they both slip a grin
and bust out laughing
the kids are fine
How are yours?

~ amba elieff

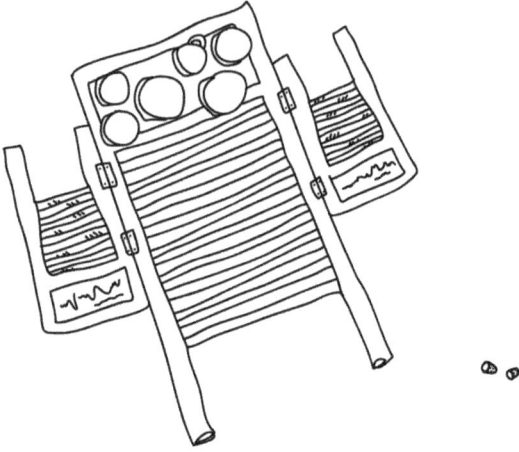

Two men playing
on the corner
a crowd gathers round
a steel national guitar
and a triple washboard player
three washboards
a large one in the center
with seven old dented tin measuring cups
attached across the top
the two smaller washboards on the sides
affixed upside down
one glass and one brass
as the introductory notes begin to play
the washboard player twists and fixes
each thimble tight
one on each finger and thumbs
then the guitar lets loose with

Jitterbug Swing
and the washboards have a life of their own
his wrists loose
the fingers dance and fly across
the corrugated centers
fluid and persistent
the thimble tipped fingers
tap, glide, stroke, caress
a carefully choreographed dance
fingers up and down
wrists twisting and turning
then fingers hopping up to beat on
measuring cups and back down
to catch the washboards
it is mesmerizing
feet are tapping, bodies bouncing
Come all you women lets do the jitterbug
swing

~ *amba elieff*

Summer
meant sunglasses
men's, women's, children's
left on the trail
normally
at the waterfalls
sitting on a stone wall
or a rock or log
I collected them
for two summers
every time I hiked
one pair
two pairs
tucked them
into my backpack
about two dozen
at home
they are displayed
on a shelf
reminders of hikes
and careless hikers

~ *amba elieff*

Pave me
said the world
streets and sidewalks
stars, flowers, circles, crosses
and
names
Hocking, Logan Block, Nelsonville
shale and fire brick clay blended
dark red, brown, purplish
fired in bee hive kilns
2000 degrees
men salt glazing
pavers indestructible
their work still visible today

~ amba elieff

He was grateful
for her white gray hair
her black hair
was always so hard
to check
for ticks
but now
the challenge
mole, mole, mole
freckle
tick

~ amba elieff

History
like braille
inside the tunnels
running fingers
slowly and gently
over the sandstone
feeling the runnels
and ridges of hand hewn
chiseled tunnels
work of men
with bandanas to protect their lungs
during a time of depression
sending checks home
unaware they were
creating a timeless treasure

~ amba elieff

Does anyone sharpen a pencil anymore?
a staple of back to school
back in the day
found in cereal boxes, gumball machines, stores
made to look like
instruments, food, guns, dinosaurs
cartoon characters
Disney, Star Wars, Barbie, Hello Kitty, Looney
Tunes, Garfield
animals, flowers, antiques
cars all different models and years
army vehicles, planes, helicopters
anything that could be shaped around the
blade of the pencil sharpener
wood, plastic, glass, metal
and
two steps into the building and immediately
you look so you can say... I had one just like this

~ amba elieff

Only memories are left
of the round cement house
a work of art by two men
Stewart and Ballinger
a prototype of a durable home
durable enough to withstand tornado or
hurricane
never finished
labeled Stewart's Folly
by locals
looking like some alien spaceship
but much too heavy to fly
believed to be
impervious to fire
until the debris inside
and maybe arson
torched it
from the inside out
the gray cement ball residing
on a garage door
til it was no more than a crumbled pile
of cement

~ *amba elieff*

A red beret
converse sneakers
handmade denim duffle bag over her shoulder
wrinkled wizened face
in her 67th year
she was going for a walk
no one questioned
she did that all the time
in the woods of Southeastern Ohio
walked
but this time
from Georgia to Maine
once, twice, three times during her life
the Appalachian Trail
to come home
and help create a small version of that trail
The Buckeye Trail
circling Ohio - the first mile
blazed blue in Hocking
and the legend goes that she bought that
first gallon of paint
dreaming the trails might one day connect

~ *amba elieff*

Candy cane smoke stack
high in the sky
visible from all over the town
it will always be
Mother Mead
no matter who owns it
the smell is the same
the smell of money
of sweat
pulp into paper
pulp into paper

~ amba elieff

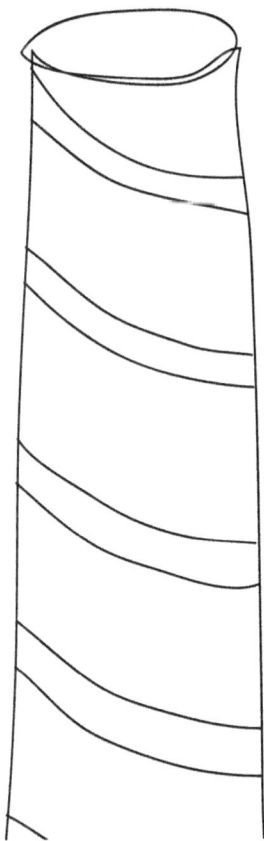

Hunting through
the piles of pavers
torn up roads
carefully reading each name
knowing that the eyes will
self correct
Nelsonville
Logan
Hocking
looking for the
backwards
"N"s
and
backwards
"K"s
sign of illiteracy
or
sign of a clever foreman
uniquely marking the bricks
from his shift
ensuring his crew gets paid
for every one

~ *amba elieff*

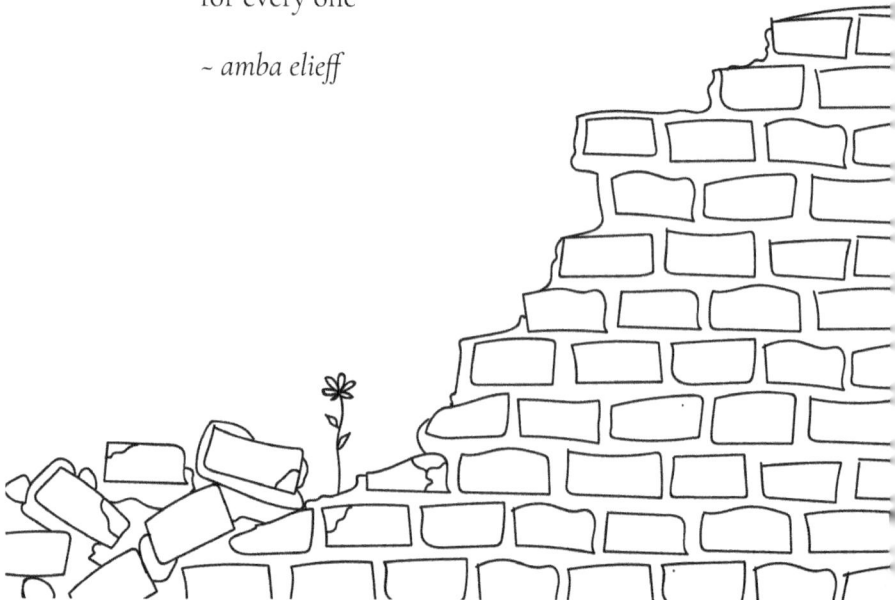

IN THE HILLS

Far away from my home in the hills
in a city
in another state
I look at the fireplace
in this 1920s house
I'm visiting
and staring up at me
a brick buff imprinted
SAVAGE
a firebrick from the hills
imperishable number 5 fire clay
withstanding heat of 2000 to 3000 degrees
made back home
in the hills
in the early 1900s
now a piece of warmth
in hearth and home

~ amba elieff

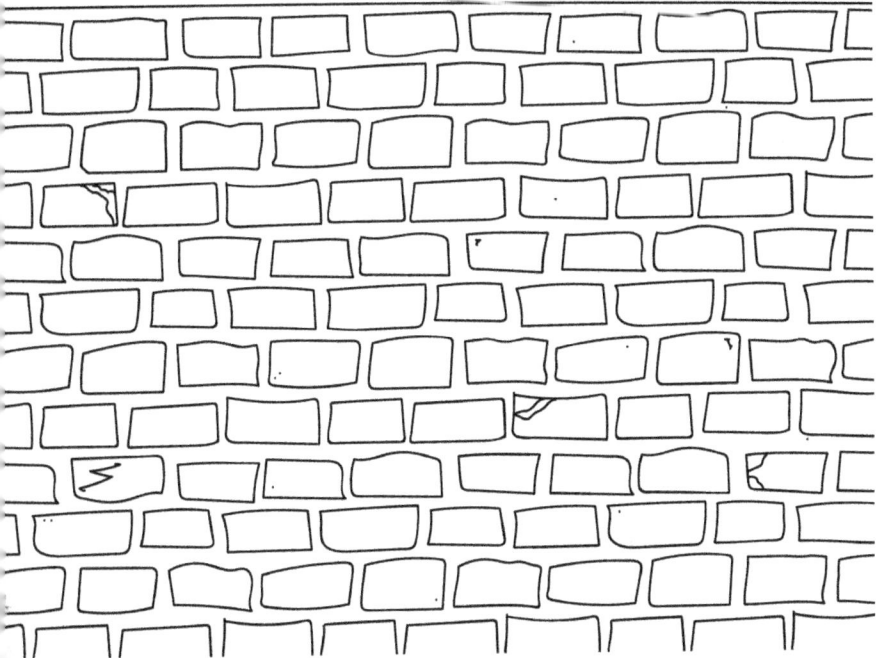

Grandma and Grandpa's
when Grandma isn't home
4 years old
big brown eyes and tow headed
wide eyed
watching everything
I follow Grandpa to the basement
Grandma's wringer washer
the shower
and along the back wall
hidden in the dark
shiny copper
Grandpa lifts his finger
to his lips
whispers
don't tell Grandma
I close my lips tight
I look up
at the snaking coil of copper tubes
like the crazy straw
from my cherry icy
my eyes follow it down
to a little straight pipe
where water dripped
my eyes rest there
drip, drip, drip
into the bucket
Grandpa whispers
moonshine

~ *amba elieff*
inspired by Missy (Waldie) Mullins

IN THE HILLS

She knew
how to make moonshine
she made it everyday
but it wasn't
Grandpa's moonshine

~ *amba elieff*
inspired by Missy (Waldie) Mullins

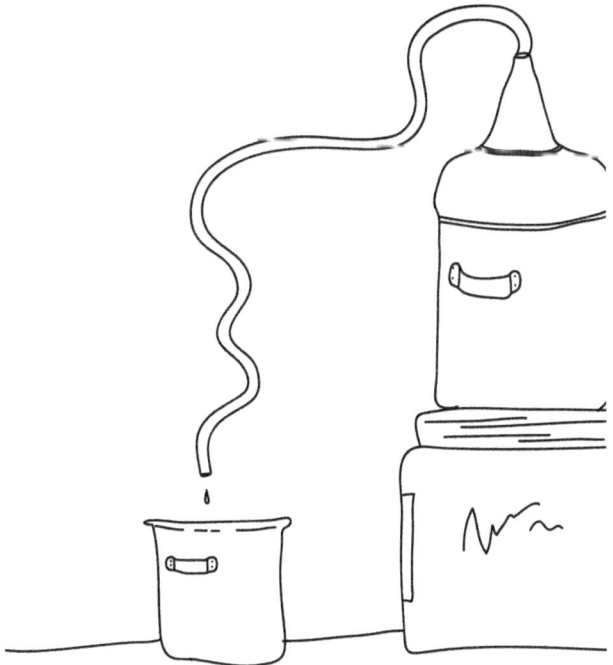

She kept a mouse log
every mouse she caught
she named before she released it
into the world
like hurricanes and tropical storms
she only used humane traps
no glue sheet torture
no poison to later kill
the hunted mouse
and
the hunter owl or hawk or fox
instead released
in a field or the woods
where the circle of life
can continue

~ *amba elieff*

IN THE HILLS

At night
the cemetery glows
I wonder at the lights
yellow, blue, green, amber, white
sprinkled all over
amongst the tombstones
I imagine they might be
multi-colored fireflies
hovering close to the ground
stationary
sentinels
for those that we miss

~ *amba elieff*

IN THE HILLS

He was an honest small town cop
a good cop
with a wife
with a friend
with a copper still
with a moonshine recipe
with spring fed water
with an idea

He was a distiller
and a cop
with a wife
with a partner
hauling water
making mash out of corn
selling moonshine

She was his wife
an unfaithful wife
with a lover
was his partner
was his friend
with a recipe for powder
with a distillery front
to distribute
with an idea

IN THE HILLS

The DEA showed up
a bug
a sting
a warrant
confiscation

He was a distiller cop
innocent
confused
shut down

The distiller cop
with a new distillery
no wife
no partner
just a story to tell

~ amba elieff
inspired by Brian St. Clair

Her resume
was simple
fourth generation
moonshiner

~ amba elieff
inspired by Missy (Waldie) Mullins

I love seeing
the blue blazes
some of them
I know by heart
I have hiked the trails
so many times
but still
I feel the urge
and I rest my hand
on the trunk
of a tree
next to the blaze
and for a moment
I acknowledge that
I am part
of Grandma Gatewood's
legacy

~ *amba elieff*

He was executed
by the sun
solar panels
on the roof
of the prison

~ *amba elieff*

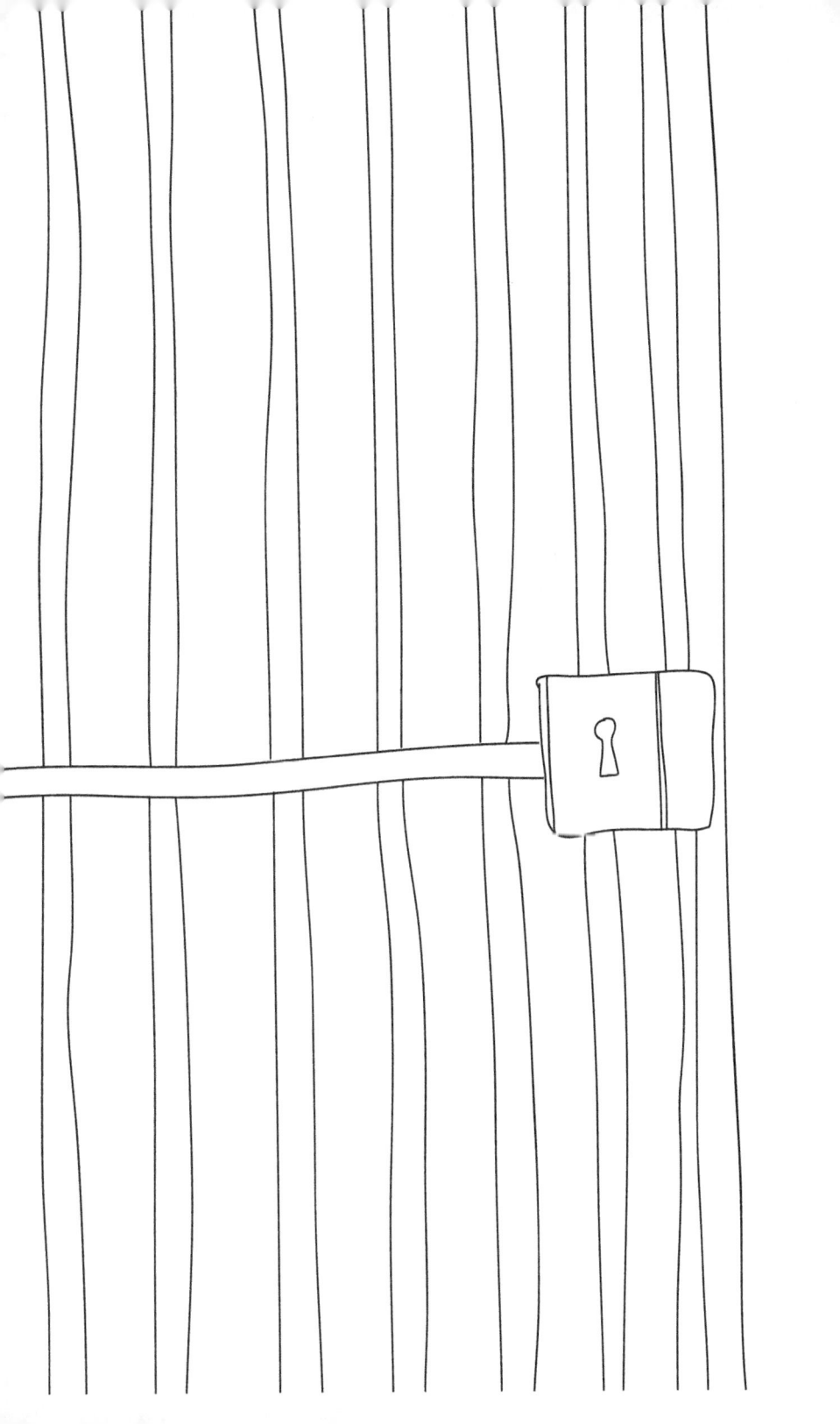

IN THE HILLS

We were hiking
her land
on Peach Ridge
doing a reconnaissance
planning a future hike
for Touch the Earth Adventures
many years since she had
visited this land
for her
everything looked familiar
until it didn't
which turn did she miss
no worries
we were hikers
machetes in hand
to break trail
backpacks with water and snacks but
if we wander too far the wrong way we
disappear
into the back end
of Strouds Run
Twenty six hundred acres of wooded forest
it is late afternoon
on a rise there is a cell phone signal
she calls
phone rings no answer
another number
she knows everyone
on this ridge
more rings and an answer
the request
go out to your car and honk the horn

IN THE HILLS

we are lost
might have heard something
honk again
we start walking
toward the sound
keep honking every 5 minutes
and she hangs up
through brambles
and honeysuckle
we stumble
still following the sound
it is dusk
we listen to that glorious sound
as we walk out of the woods
driveway is filled with people
five more minutes
and we were coming in
to find you

~ *amba elieff*

We all migrate
from cities
to this place
where we find
peace
we want a slower life
we want to breathe
we want to see
the stars at night
listen to the rushing water
that isn't flowing into
a storm sewer

we want to watch
the hills play
hide and seek
in the fog
while we play
hide and seek
with the city

~ *amba elieff*

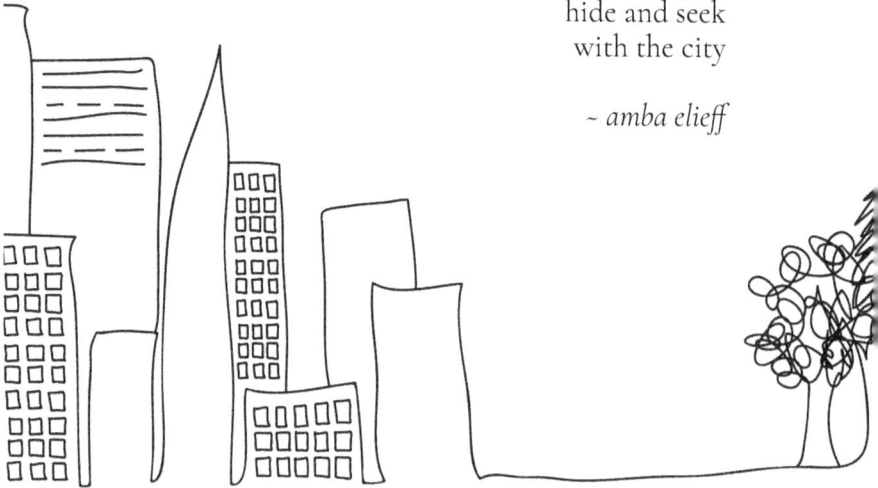

The Mead
generations of workers
generations of opportunity
buying houses
that became homes
paying for babies and braces
and college educations
making family
from co-workers
a chance to be
middle class
in a small town
proud of a day's work
another roll of paper
down the line
the mill bigger than
the smokestack
supporting diners, shops, bookstores,
bars, a library
a town

~ *amba elieff*

The coal mine still burns
deep underground
a message from striking miners
trying to organize
for safety and a fair wage
in Robinson's cave they met
hidden and secluded
acoustics that allowed
men to be heard
space that allowed
men to gather
1884
those men had no idea
that mine would still
be burning today
ground collapses, smoke, steam,
and fireholes
reminders of our past

Would we be brave enough
to do that today?

~ amba elieff

Small children wading
into the green water
knee deep
a waterfall pool
in the deeper water
at the base of the rock
under the waterfall
the home of a snapping turtle
as big around as a large pizza
40 years old or more
slowly swims toward
the wigging feet
mouth wide open
and a little girl screams crocodile
a rush of bodies out of the pool
looking for the monster
in the water

~ amba elieff

IN THE HILLS

It commands the corner
of the cemetery
hidden as you walk up the entrance
and
the only thing you can see
once you step off of the walkway
into the cemetery
on a hill
bark rough with age
What have you seen?
Who was here around 1425?
when your acorn
buried by a squirrel
sprouted up into the world
Native Americans peopled the land
Columbus had not set sail
you saw the invasion of the white man,
the wars,
the mistreatment of people and land
and now you see me touching you
and wondering
How old were you when the children
started climbing you?
Are there initials carved by lovers
way up high?
Are you sad that no others survived
the centuries with you?
Did the bodies down below
make you strong and protect you?
When I am gone, will you remember
I was here?

~ amba elieff

IN THE HILLS

THE WONDER

IN THE HILLS

Its massive branches
sweep toward the ground
each branch as large as
the trunk of the surrounding trees
shagbark hickory, oaks, and maples
far younger but old in their own right
like young groupies
admiring the aged one
over 600 years old
watched each of those youngsters grow
parented many of the oaks
a community of trees
waiting for more wisdom
from the elder

~ *amba elieff*

In the hills
pines own the smell of the air
and the softness on the ground
but the hemlocks
own the light
the blue green light
that only appears
when
the sunlight
radiates down through the hemlock branches
making the world
a part of their magic

~ amba elieff

Snow is the tears
when mother nature laughs
and
the icicles
are her laughter

~ *amba elieff*

I want to live in a world
full of ridges and gorges and hollers
where the creek is as long as a river
where the largest washboard in the world
watches over the town
and a pencil sharpener museum
welcomes you
apples are all mouthwatering
daughters inherit the farm
and roads have names
like Happy Hollow, Goat Run Honey Fork,
Sauerkraut Ridge, and Blackjack
and everything moves slow

there is time to chat, shoot the breeze, jaw
for awhile
at the local store

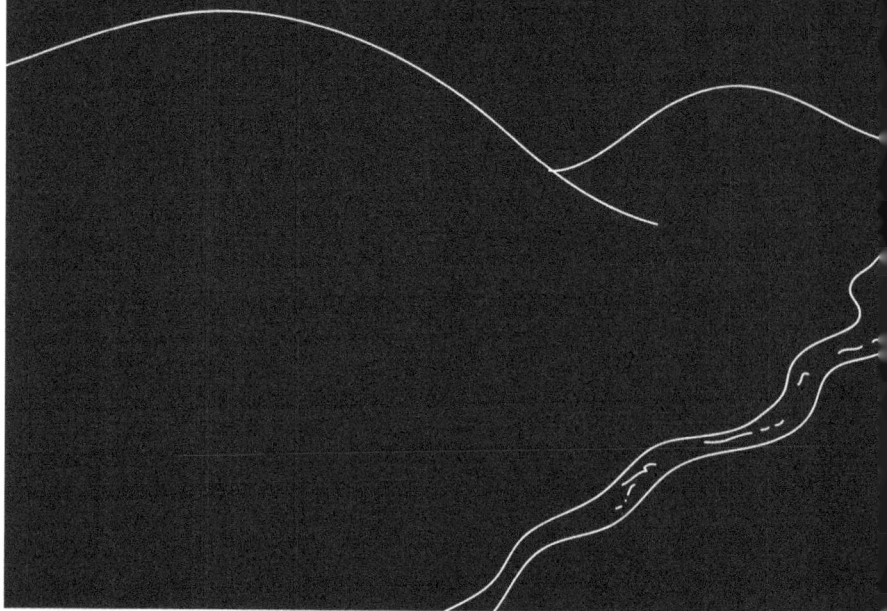

tall tales like sasquatch are real
stars glitter like diamonds
in a pitch dark sky
filled with the milky way
and owls tell you good night
while the mice scurry
into your basement to hide
and the sun rises
in the gorge
a half hour after everyone
on the ridge is up and awake
sun in their eyes
still dark below
this is my Mayberry

~ amba elieff

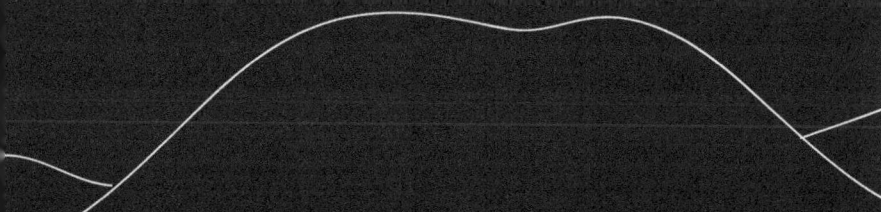

IN THE HILLS

The mice visited while I was away
the cast iron skillet
left out
greased on the stove
black as night
slick and shiny with lard
so the mouse droppings
are nearly invisible
but the top of the stove
between the burners
in the vast center inbetween
black as night
a piece of artwork
tiny greasy paw prints
it looks like it was a party
a dance floor
delicate intricate patterns
like the frost on a window in the winter
a lacey calling card
letting me know they are there

~ amba elieff

The silence
is more quiet here
in the woods
in the cabin
early morning
as the light
begins seeping
into the day
more quiet
the day not yet awake
the loud cacophony
of the night
wood frogs
calling and mating
now silent
early March
they make the water boil
with their bouncing
frisky, rolling, cavorting bodies
and spring peepers
singing
their noise so much more than their size
another week temperature a constant 55
from across the farmer's field
toads
their own mating rituals begin
and I revel in it all
the quiet and the orgies
the life in the woods

~ amba elieff

Trundling across the road
one small movement
at a time
so so soooo slowly
it looks more like
cumbersome dragging
scooting
than walking

my eyes are always
scanning the road
human is their
main predator
I want to be their
savior
and I see him ahead
I stop on the side
of the road
hazards on
pluck him from the asphalt
and move him to the edge of the woods
that was his destination
I admire his amazing shell
yellow sunburst
the size of my hand
set him down
and watch him trundle on

~ *amba elieff*

IN THE HILLS

I see the light
on the hills
shadows
from the clouds
all the newborn greens
and my heart sighs

~ *amba elieff*

The fiddleheads
light and dusky green
with a fine white fuzz
like fur
waiting to become ferns
when the fronds open
their fiddlehead selves
will the forest hear
sweet violin sounds
as they slowly unfurl

- amba elieff

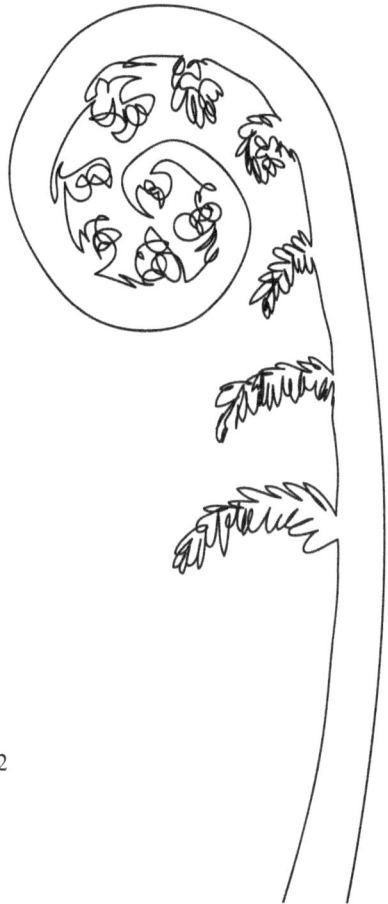

IN THE HILLS

I opened the window
the warm night air
caresses my body
spring
I look out at the dark night
stars glittering above
I hear the chorus of frogs
cricket frogs and wood frogs
in the vernal pool
boys calling girls
and I drift off to sleep
serenaded by their orgy

~ *amba elieff*

There is a party
in the vernal pool
welcoming me home
as my headlights
illuminate
a frog hopping
across my path
heading
for the pool

- amba elieff

Early spring
redbud blooms
tiny deep pink flowers
thick on the branches
explosions of color
demanding all the attention
like a new lover
wooing the spring
into summer
flowers gone
now
it's hearts are
on it's sleeve

~ *amba elieff*

She couldn't decide
which was more sad
the melancholy sad
of the old homes and buildings
slowly deteriorating
owners no longer able to manage upkeep
or
the gut wrenching sad
of the bright shiny
new buildings
taking their places
and all the charm

~ *amba elieff*

Light is just
beginning
early morning
a sacred time
peaceful
just me and the forest
the falls and the sandstone
a handful of pigeons
the water falls
like a baptism
I sit on a rock
near the pool
the water splashes me
I look up
the first rays
of sunshine
break through
the hemlocks
revealing tiny rainbows
in every droplet

~ *amba elieff*

IN THE HILLS

The cold lingered
well into April
my breath
a cloud
mingling
with the fog
early morning hike
with the dog
both of us
trying to
warm up
looking for the sun
as my gaze travels up
from my feet on uneven ground
dutchman's breeches with lacy leaves
hepatica with its spots and tiny flowers
giant white trillium blooms still small
jack-in-the-pulpit standing straight and tall
all sprinkle the hillside
with the backdrop of sandstone
and redbud bursting deep pink knots
I stop looking for the sun

- *amba elieff*

Cabin in the woods
always trapping mice
every night the ritual
traps with peanut butter
placed in the basement
check them in the morning
a good night
three traps two mice
I load the traps in the car
we are going for a ride
I take them to the astronomy park
far enough away
a permanent vacation from my home
I drop their two wriggling brown bodies
into the meadow
it looks like
they are swimming through the tall green
grass
tall if you are a mouse
they work their way through
looking for a place to hide
I think they will be
hunkered down
waiting for dark
when they can stargaze

~ *amba elieff*

141

The toads are singing
in the low flooded section
of the farmer's field
I can't see them
but I can hear them
their sweet trilling
overwhelming
the waning frog song
in the vernal pool
a turtle is sunning
on a log in the creek
spice bush and redbud in bloom
pollen so thick
on the deck
it looks like sawdust
it is finally spring

~ *amba elieff*

IN THE HILLS

Don't touch
Don't move
everything in the earth
in the air
in this one spot
allows
the pink lady slipper
hanging from a stem
tucked in the wood
on a hillside
to live
almost 50 years old
1, 2, 3, 4, 5, 6, 7
8, 9, 10, 11, 12, 13, 14
15, or more years
then maybe a new plant will bloom

~ amba elieff

Old's Hollow trail
with it's hidden cemetery
what remains
of the people of Hope
now under the lake
they worked
the iron furnace
still standing
another type of tombstone
I watch the blue heron
glide into the water
graceful with those long legs
hunting lunch
I wander
toward the spring bloomers
covering the hillsides
that roll into the creek
trilliums white and red
foam flower mingles with yellow bellwort
splashes of phlox a jack-in-the-pulpit
the display
kisses the eyes
while a pileated
drums a welcome

~ amba elieff

I miss the days
before cell phone service
morning at the cabins
at the state park
visitors
outside
weekend away
not able to unplug
wander up the small rise
and to the back of the cabin
to the parking lot
staring at the screen
raising the phone up
to the left
to the right
like the phone is doing
calisthenics
the person
not understanding
that they have left
that connected world
and entered the world
of nature

~ *amba elieff*

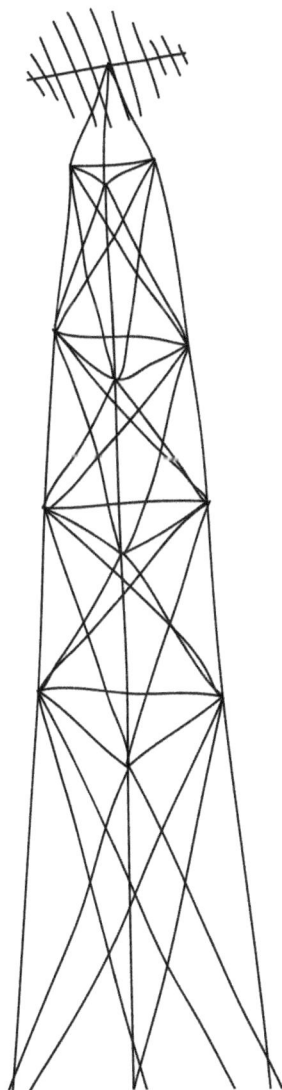

IN THE HILLS

I have a dream
of never needing to leave
to bury my roots
next to the hemlocks
let my body sluice
on the water of the creeks
and my mind having endless
afternoons
for reading on a rock
in the middle
of everything

~ amba elieff

Deep in the woods
along a creek
the spindly trees
reach for the sun
leaves large, long, and rounded
like something from a tropical rainforest
biding time
flowers in April deep maroon bells that
stare at the ground
it takes two trees to get that flower
they can't use their own pollen
then the fruit grows
a lime green potato shaped thing
no bigger than the palm of your hand
biding time
for the fruit to fall
pick it hard and green - the pawpaw is
worthless
it won't finish ripening off the tree
but when it falls grab it quick
the animals are waiting too
and
pawpaws will be gone
in the blink of your eye

~ *amba elieff*

I look over the prairie
late summer
blooms of joe pye, ironweed, wingstem
bees buzzing
gathering nectar
for the hive
my eyes can't soak up enough
of the majestic beauty
flowers and grass as tall as me
as I try to memorize this tapestry
of color
I realize
there is much more grass than flower
and
if it wasn't for the
grass
the flowers would have no backdrop
to make their beauty shine

~ *amba elieff*

Snow is joyful, happy rain

~ amba elieff

IN THE HILLS

To be a drop of water
part of a waterfall
part of a raging
flow of water
to fling yourself
over the edge
with abandon
now separate
sparkling in the light
flying through the air
a drop
no fear
trusting the water
below
will catch you
and return you home

~ *amba elieff*

I really wanted honeycrisp apples
the best honeycrisp
are always from
Laurelville Fruit Farm
three generations of apples
three daughters now run the farm
open since 1912
making cider
selling apples, peaches, plums
and it is toward the end of the season
and the honeycrisp are all gone
I stare at the bags
of apples
varieties I have never seen
he sees me staring
my face crinkled
and he tells me
the evercrisp
it is a sweetheart of an apple
and now
I look forward
every year
for my evercrisps

~ *amba elieff*

IN THE HILLS

In the dark night
lights glow amongst the dead
they look like
fairies floating
blue, turquoise, red, amber, white
a cemetery
filled with love and remembrance

~ amba elieff

A girl in the hills
every year
as the ice under the waterfall
builds
she visits
each week
waiting
for the magical moment
when the huge mound of ice
turns blue
as close as a small town girl
will ever get to a glacier
pictures she has seen in magazines
her blue ice magic
right here

~ amba elieff

I had a dream
I told everyone
who would listen
a cabin
amongst the hemlocks
and sandstone
to live in that cabin
and I nursed that dream
always looking for the place
until I thought it was only
a fantasy
an embarrassment
that I told everyone
until
a night with a star filled sky
black velvet night
power went off
and I knew
without that dream
a cabin
I would have no life
so
I dreamed
and chased
that cabin
and made it real

~ *amba elieff*

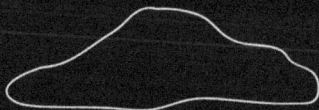

I see the mushrooms
a stand of them
all mauve pink
caps thick
some as big as
the palm of my hand
all perfect
except one
with a bite
a perfect
half circle
gone
I hear
the squirrel mom
say
you have to try it
you have to take
one bite
- *amba elieff*

IN THE HILLS

Daiquiri and beer
mayapple and foam flower
while a stand of
jack-in-the-pulpit
judges

~ *amba elieff*

The first time
I saw the seasons
of the hills
I understood
why
there were so many colors
in a crayon box

~ amba elieff

Mysteries
in the night
when
everyone is gone
flying squirrels
mingling amongst
jack-o-lantern mushrooms
glow through
the air

~ *amba elieff*

The large tulip poplar
brushes the warm blue sky
my eyes travel up the trunk
bark light and deeply grooved
I see the flowers orange and yellow
high in the branches
almost tropical
but then
the hummmmm
a split in the grooves
bees zooming in and out
I touch it
and feel their vibrations

~ amba elieff

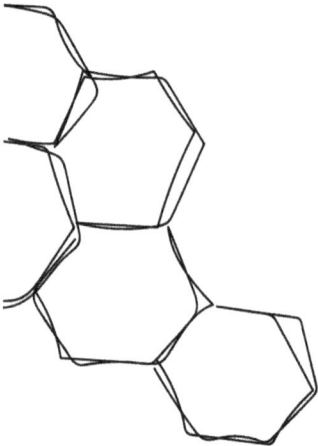

Maple trees
old and wise
in front of the school
bare
snow still on the ground
temperatures bouncing
freeze and thaw
freeze and thaw
the sap is rising
the metal buckets
are hung
collecting the pure
clear drops
looks like water
tastes sweet
it is a chemistry project
biology
history
economics
sap boiled into syrup
bottled and sold
all that learning
from the wise, old trees

~ *amba elieff*

The sky has just started brightening
early morning
a day to give thanks
to the forest
to the water
to the animals
to mother nature
a day to give thanks
for all the blessings
of the week
my church
is a cave
and a waterfall
peaceful
this early
just me
and the trees
and the water
today
it falls
with a crash
into the pool below
some days it is a quiet drip
and then it can be
a dried up silent nothing
but it is always
sacred

~ amba elieff

IN THE HILLS

Snowflakes
big, white, fluffy
floating down
into the gorge
Old Man's Cave above
golden as a desert in Arizona
below
the snow wafting through the air
as though someone shook a snow globe
and like magic
I am in the wonder
looking up from the bottom
surrounded by snow

~ *amba elieff*

IN THE HILLS

I always
want to escape
to the hills
get lost in her
deep green forest
where nothing
exists
besides me
and the hills
and the waterfalls

- amba elieff

She watches the water
tumble down
into the pool below
her mind floats back
to two small girls
in the sand
picking up milk quartz
sliding down stones
shaped like slides
butts brown
sand embedded into fibers
that won't come out
faces tilt up toward
that falling water
feeling the spray
giggling
joy and wonder
all in an afternoon

~ amba elieff

165

IN THE HILLS

ABOUT THE AUTHOR

Amba Elieff is from a small town in Ohio sandwiched between Cincinnati and Dayton. She lived there 50 years, which included growing up, attending Miami University at the community campus in town, marriage, raising children, divorce, and a good corporate job. During that time she wrote poetry in journals capturing all the experiences in her life. Not a grand and exciting life. A simple ordinary life full of extraordinary moments. Moments that most people recognize like an old friend letting them know that they aren't alone.

Today she lives with her husband and two dogs in Kentucky waiting to move to the home of her heart in Hocking Hills.

This is her fourth volume of poetry. Maiden Mother Crone was published in 2022, Domesticated Demons in 2023, and Naked & Healing in 2024.

You can learn more about Amba Elieff, order copies of other volumes, and check out her merch, at her website, https://ambapoetry.com.

IG: @amba.elieff

IN THE HILLS

ABOUT THE ILLUSTRATOR

When people ask Gabrielle Scarlett what she does for a living, she says that she "makes things pretty." She spends her work hours (and the personal ones, too) creating art in a variety of forms - from the physical kind that can hang on your wall, to websites and strategic brand suites for small business owners.

She now lives in Edinburgh, Scotland with her fiancé, but grew up in the same Ohio town as Amba, her mother. Despite now living halfway across the world, she thinks daily of her adventures in Hocking and Vinton counties with her family growing up, and she likes to think the connection with nature these fostered shows in her body of work to this day.

You can learn more about Gabrielle on her website, https://gabriellescarlett.com.

IG: @thegabriellescarlett

www.ingramcontent.com/pod-product-compliance
Lightning Source LLC
Chambersburg PA
CBHW021620270326
41931CB00008B/789